# Eco-Logical Brain Games

## Tony J. Tallarico

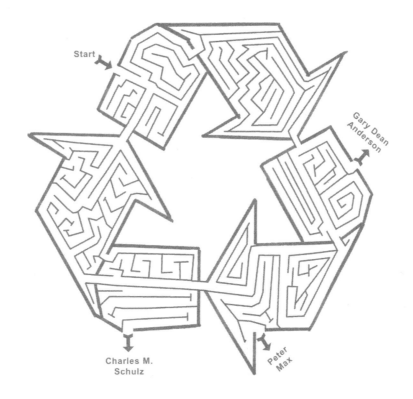

Start →

Gary Dean Anderson →

Charles M. Schulz

Peter Max

**Dover Publications, Inc.**
**Mineola, New York**

**Planet Friendly Publishing**
✔ Made in the United States
✔ Printed on Recycled Paper
Learn more at www.greenedition.org

At Dover Publications we're committed to producing books in an earth-friendly manner and to helping our customers make greener choices.

Manufacturing books in the United States ensures compliance with strict environmental laws and eliminates the need for international freight shipping, a major contributor to global air pollution.

And printing on recycled paper helps minimize our consumption of trees, water and fossil fuels. The text of *Eco-Logical Brain Games* was printed on paper made with 30% post-consumer waste, and the cover was printed on paper made with 10% post-consumer waste. According to Environmental Defense's Paper Calculator, by using these innovative papers instead of conventional papers, we achieved the following environmental benefits:

Trees Saved: 11 • Air Emissions Eliminated: 863 pounds
Water Saved: 4,638 gallons • Solid Waste Eliminated: 282 pounds

For more information on our environmental practices, please visit us online at www.doverpublications.com/green

*Copyright*

Copyright © 2009 by Tony J. Tallarico
All rights reserved.

*Bibliographical Note*

*Eco-Logical Brain Games* is a new work, first published by Dover Publications, Inc., in 2009.

*International Standard Book Number*
*ISBN-13: 978-0-486-46840-2*
*ISBN-10: 0-486-46840-2*

Manufactured in the United States by Courier Corporation
46840202
**www.doverpublications.com**

# Note

What happens when you combine fascinating facts about ecology with lots of challenging puzzles? You have a terrific way to discover one of the biggest issues of our time: threats to our environment. In this unique book, you'll find out about recycling, Earth's ecosystems, the rainforest, pollution, and other topics as you complete mazes, do word searches, solve codes, find hidden objects, as well as many other fun activities. From tips on how to save energy to information about careers in ecology, you'll find each page packed with things to do and learn. There is a Solutions section beginning on page 36, if you want to check your answers, too. Are you ready? Let's get started on these "eco-logical" brain games!

# A GLOBAL OBSERVANCE

**Earth Day is celebrated in many countries each year on April 22. The day helps inspire awareness of and appreciation for our Earth's environment. The date is also important because it is the birthday of a famous agriculturist.**

Travel through this letter maze by choosing the path made up of only letters from the phrase -
**SAVE OUR PLANET**
(Hint: The letters will be used more than once and will not appear in any particular order.)

**START**

# A HIDDEN MESSAGE

Write these words in alphabetical order into the puzzle grid. The fourth letter of each word will help spell out a hidden message.

HIDDEN
MESSAGE
↓

STAGE

CRATE

WHINE

TRIED

MERIT

UNDER

PLANK

ITCHY

RISKY

TEARY

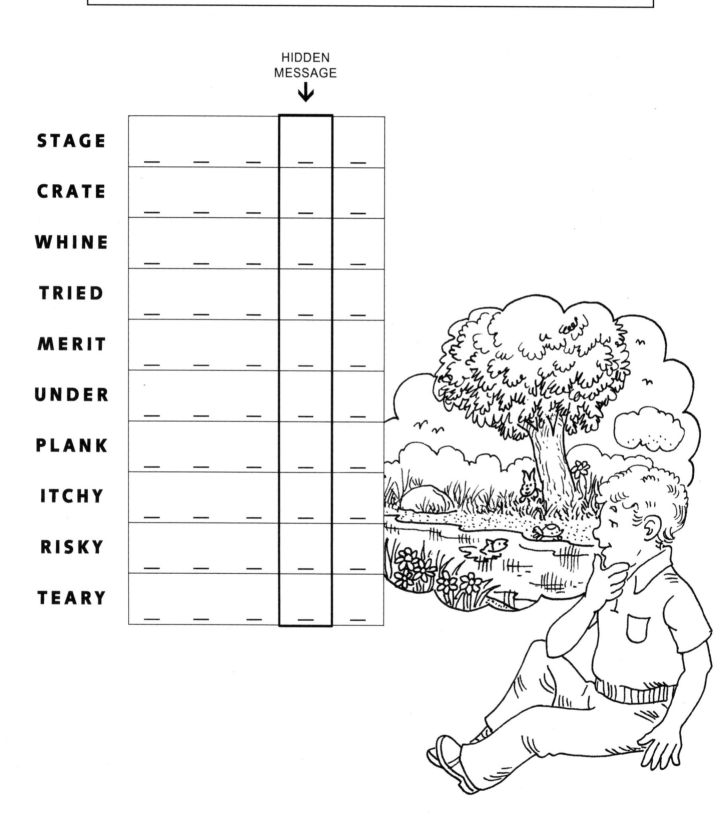

2

# A NEW IDEA

**Our landfills are filling up with old asphalt shingles (the material used to cover roofs of houses). To reduce the landfill waste, a few companies are recycling the shingles into a useful product.**

Find and circle the following ten words (having to do with a home's roof) in the puzzle below. The letters that remain, once listed in the order they appear, will spell out the hidden phrase.

- ○ **ASPHALT**
- ○ **COLOR**
- ○ **INSTALL**
- ○ **INSULATE**
- ○ **METAL**
- ○ **SLATE**
- ○ **SLOPE**
- ○ **STEEP**
- ○ **STYLE**
- ○ **TILE**

```
I  P  A  E  L  I  T  E
N  S  M  E  T  A  L  T
S  T  Y  L  E  V  A  A
T  E  I  N  G  R  H  L
A  E  M  A  T  O  P  U
L  P  E  T  A  L  S  S
L  E  R  I  A  O  A  N
E  P  O  L  S  C  L  I
```

### SHINGLES ARE BEING RECYCLED INTO:

\_\_ \_\_ \_\_ \_\_ \_\_ \_\_ \_\_ \_\_  \_\_ \_\_ \_\_ \_\_ \_\_ \_\_

# A SPECIAL MESSAGE

Using a pencil,
darken in the areas that
contain a dot ●
to reveal a
special message.

# A WARMER EARTH?

Earth has warmed by about one degree
Fahrenheit over the past 100 years.
The Earth might be getting warmer on its own,
but many scientists think that
things people do are causing this change.

What is the phrase that is commonly used to refer to
Earth's climate changes?
Answer each clue below. The circled letters,
written in the exact order they appear,
will spell out the phrase.

| Clue | |
|---|---|
| A young female | ◯ _ _ ◯ |
| A sphere of planet Earth | _ _ ◯◯ _ |
| Fourth month | ◯ _ _ _ ◯ |
| Opposite of strong | ◯ _ ◯ _ |
| To wander or ramble | ◯ _ _ ◯ |
| Last meal of the day | _ ◯ _ ◯ _ _ |
| Fuel for car | ◯ _ _ _ |

_ _ _ _ _ _ _ _ _ _ _ _ _

# ABSORBING POLLUTANTS

An average tree can absorb pollutants from the air - such as ozone and nitrogen oxides. How many pounds of pollutants from the air can a typical tree absorb in just one year?

Follow this number maze to add up to exactly **50** to reach the correct answer.

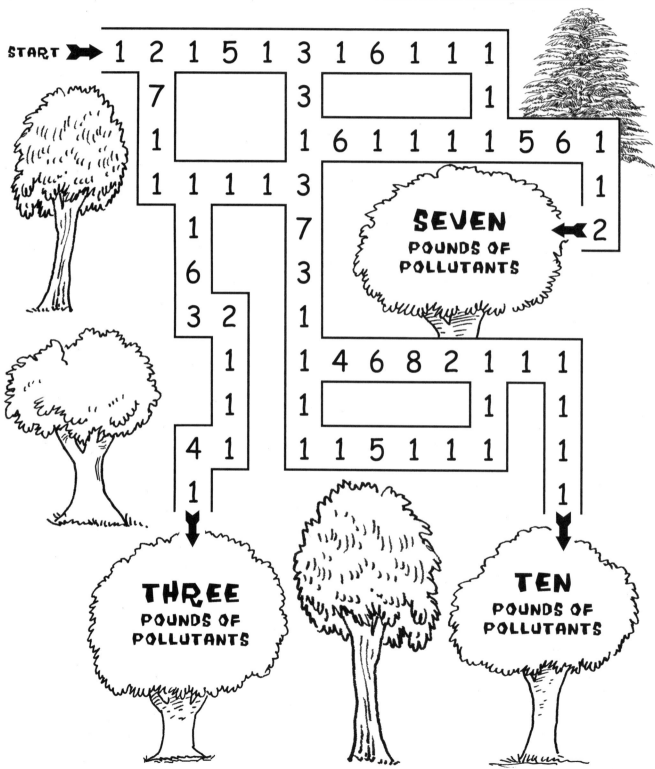

# AN EARLY TREE

One of the earliest-known modern trees first appeared 370 million years ago!
It looked similar to a Christmas tree and quickly covered most parts of
the Earth with its first forests.

To learn the name of this tree, cross out each letter that appears **THREE** times in this puzzle grid.
List the remaining letters, in the order they appear, in the blank spaces below.

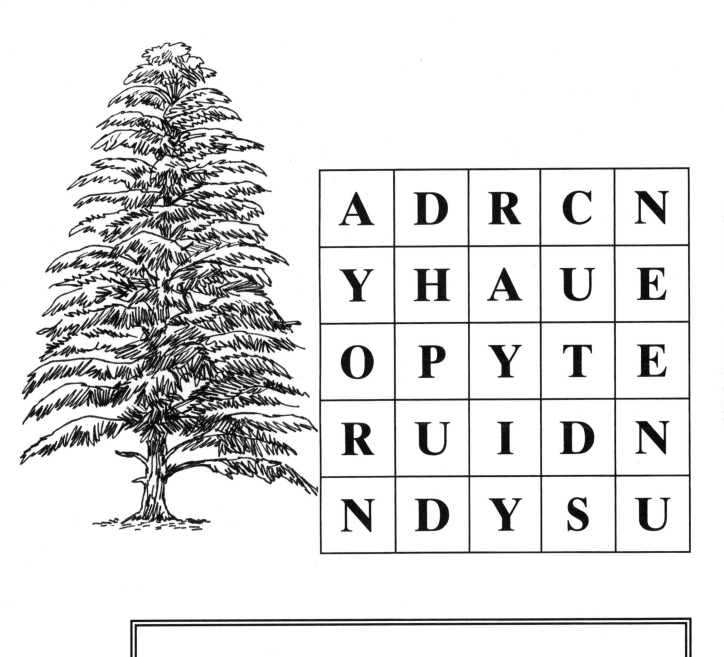

| A | D | R | C | N |
|---|---|---|---|---|
| Y | H | A | U | E |
| O | P | Y | T | E |
| R | U | I | D | N |
| N | D | Y | S | U |

_ _ _ _ _ _ _ _ _ _ _ _ _ _ _ _ _ _ _ _

# AN INVISIBLE POLLUTANT

**Smog hanging over our cities is the most familiar form of air pollution. But there are different kinds of air pollution, some visible ... some invisible!**

> Cross out all the ODD-NUMBERED letters that appear in the boxes below. Then write the remaining EVEN-NUMBERED letters, in the order they appear, in the blank spaces. You will spell out the name of an odorless, colorless gas.

| | | | | | | |
|---|---|---|---|---|---|---|
| 7 S | 21 A | 12 C | 13 R | 11 G | 4 A | 15 N |
| 22 R | 3 H | 17 O | 2 B | 14 O | 19 I | 3 R |
| 7 B | 10 N | 2 M | 5 C | 1 E | 8 O | 24 N |
| 16 O | 11 D | 9 E | 7 N | 20 X | 9 P | 11 C |
| 5 F | 6 I | 13 H | 8 D | 19 E | 25 B | 3 N |
| 25 T | 17 Y | 23 M | 1 N | 15 F | 2 E | 21 A |

Write the remaining EVEN-NUMBERED letters here:

__ __ __ __ __ __   __ __ __ __ __ __ __

# CLEAN AIR ON THE ROAD

**Did you know that a car with a dirty air filter is more than just unhealthy?**

To learn more, use this chart to decode the following fact.

| A | C | D | E | F | G | H | I | K | L |
|---|---|---|---|---|---|---|---|---|---|
| 12 | 4 | 20 | 13 | 6 | 17 | 2 | 19 | 15 | 7 |

| M | N | O | R | S | T | U | W | Y | Z |
|---|---|---|---|---|---|---|---|---|---|
| 3 | 16 | 8 | 18 | 11 | 10 | 14 | 1 | 9 | 5 |

—— —— ——     —— —— —— ——     —— ——     ——
10  2  13      17  14  16  15      19  16      12

—— —— —— —— —— —— ——     —— —— ——
 4   7   8  17  17  13  20      12  19  18

—— —— —— —— —— ——     —— —— —— ——
 6  19   7  10  13  18       1  19   7   7

—— —— ——     —— —— —— ——     —— ——
 4  14  10      20   8   1  16       8  16

—— —— ——     —— —— —— —— —— —— ——
17  12  11       3  19   7  13  12  17  13 .

# CLEAN ENERGY

**Solar energy is energy from the sun. Today it is possible to capture the sun's heat and light and turn it into electricity, heating, and lighting. To discover the name of a device that can harness the sun's energy, follow the directions below.**

Write the name of each of these objects. One letter from each word will spell out the name of a device which can collect and convert energy into electricity!

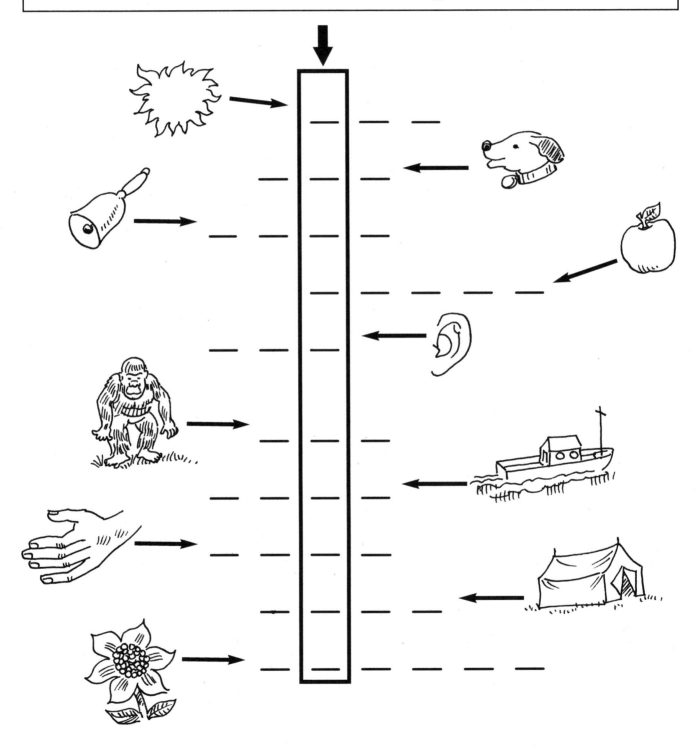

# COLOR OUR WORLD

Unscramble the names of these colors. A letter from each will spell out the hidden message.

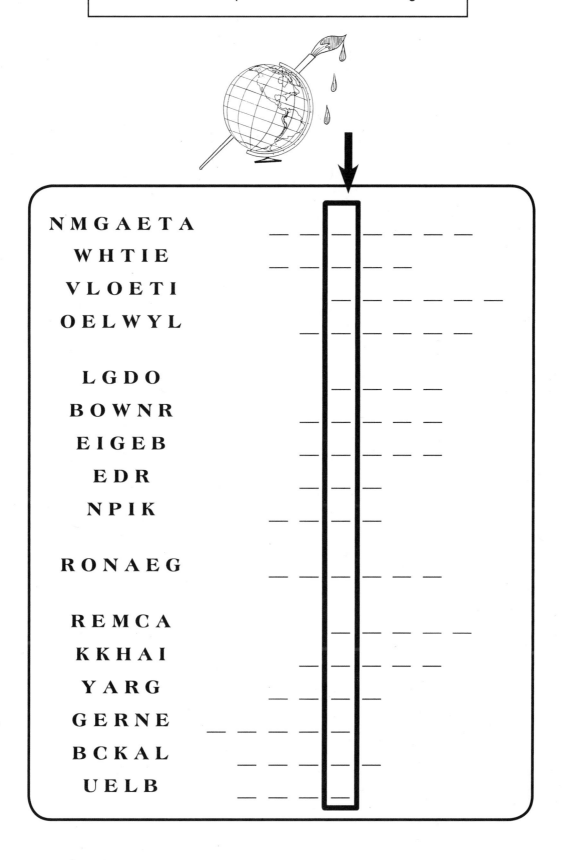

N M G A E T A     _ _ _ _ _ _ _

W H T I E    _ _ _ _ _

V L O E T I    _ _ _ _ _ _

O E L W Y L    _ _ _ _ _ _

L G D O    _ _ _ _

B O W N R    _ _ _ _ _

E I G E B    _ _ _ _ _

E D R    _ _ _

N P I K    _ _ _ _

R O N A E G    _ _ _ _ _ _

R E M C A    _ _ _ _ _

K K H A I    _ _ _ _ _

Y A R G    _ _ _ _

G E R N E    _ _ _ _ _

B C K A L    _ _ _ _ _

U E L B    _ _ _ _

# COMBO PUZZLE

Add the correct vowels (A, E, I, O, U) to these words. (The clues will help you.) Then find and circle the words in the puzzle below.

| __ __ R T H  D __ Y | W __ L D __ R N __ S S |
|---|---|
| (April 22 observance) | (Natural environment not affected by humans) |
| R __ C Y C L __ N G | T R __ __ S |
| (Reprocessing old materials into new products) | (Woody plants with branches) |
| N __ B R __ S K __ | __ N __ R G Y |
| (U.S. state where Arbor Day originated) | (Kinetic, thermal or nuclear, for example) |

```
S  S  E  N  R  E  D  L  I  W
A  D  A  Y  E  A  R  T  H  I
K  N  R  E  C  Y  C  L  N  L
S  E  T  B  Y  N  E  G  Y  D
A  Y  H  R  C  T  A  G  S  R
R  T  D  T  L  R  R  R  R  N
B  H  A  R  I  E  T  E  B  E
E  A  Y  T  N  G  D  N  E  S
N  E  B  E  G  Y  Y  E  N  S
```

# DID YOU KNOW?

Write the opposite of each of these words.
Then write the numbered letters in the correct spaces below to complete the sentence.

WEST $\overline{\phantom{x}}_{2}$ $\overline{\phantom{x}}_{21}$ $\overline{\phantom{x}}_{14}$ $\overline{\phantom{x}}_{19}$

LEFT $\overline{\phantom{x}}_{6}$ $\overline{\phantom{x}}_{18}$ $\overline{\phantom{x}}_{11}$ $\overline{\phantom{x}}_{5}$ $\overline{\phantom{x}}_{17}$

TRUE $\overline{\phantom{x}}_{22}$ $\overline{\phantom{x}}_{12}$ $\overline{\phantom{x}}_{8}$ $\overline{\phantom{x}}_{24}$ $\overline{\phantom{x}}_{1}$

OPEN $\overline{\phantom{x}}_{7}$ $\overline{\phantom{x}}_{20}$ $\overline{\phantom{x}}_{15}$ $\overline{\phantom{x}}_{4}$ $\overline{\phantom{x}}_{9}$

TALL $\overline{\phantom{x}}_{13}$ $\overline{\phantom{x}}_{23}$ $\overline{\phantom{x}}_{10}$ $\overline{\phantom{x}}_{3}$ $\overline{\phantom{x}}_{16}$

T H E $\underset{1}{\rule{1em}{0.4pt}}$ N $\underset{2}{\rule{1em}{0.4pt}}$ $\underset{3}{\rule{1em}{0.4pt}}$ G Y    W E $\underset{4}{\rule{1em}{0.4pt}}$ A V E

W $\underset{5}{\rule{1em}{0.4pt}}$ E N    W E $\underset{6}{\rule{1em}{0.4pt}}$ E $\underset{7}{\rule{1em}{0.4pt}}$ Y C $\underset{8}{\rule{1em}{0.4pt}}$ $\underset{9}{\rule{1em}{0.4pt}}$

$\underset{10}{\rule{1em}{0.4pt}}$ N E $\underset{11}{\rule{1em}{0.4pt}}$ L $\underset{12}{\rule{1em}{0.4pt}}$ $\underset{13}{\rule{1em}{0.4pt}}$ $\underset{14}{\rule{1em}{0.4pt}}$    B $\underset{15}{\rule{1em}{0.4pt}}$ $\underset{16}{\rule{1em}{0.4pt}}$ $\underset{17}{\rule{1em}{0.4pt}}$ L E

I S    E N O U G H    T O    R U N

A    R E G U L A R    L $\underset{18}{\rule{1em}{0.4pt}}$ G H $\underset{19}{\rule{1em}{0.4pt}}$

B U $\underset{20}{\rule{1em}{0.4pt}}$ B    F O R    $\underset{21}{\rule{1em}{0.4pt}}$ B O U T

$\underset{22}{\rule{1em}{0.4pt}}$ O U R    $\underset{23}{\rule{1em}{0.4pt}}$ O U R $\underset{24}{\rule{1em}{0.4pt}}$ !

# DISHWASHER FACT

Energy Star dishwashers, which use about one-third less water than non-Energy Star models, are designed to clean so well that prerinsing is not needed! Do you know someone who "cleans" their dishes before placing them in the dishwasher?

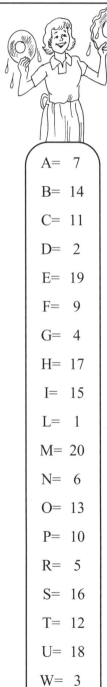

Use the chart below to decode the fact to the right.

A= 7

B= 14

C= 11

D= 2

E= 19

F= 9

G= 4

H= 17

I= 15

L= 1

M= 20

N= 6

O= 13

P= 10

R= 5

S= 16

T= 12

U= 18

W= 3

Y= 8

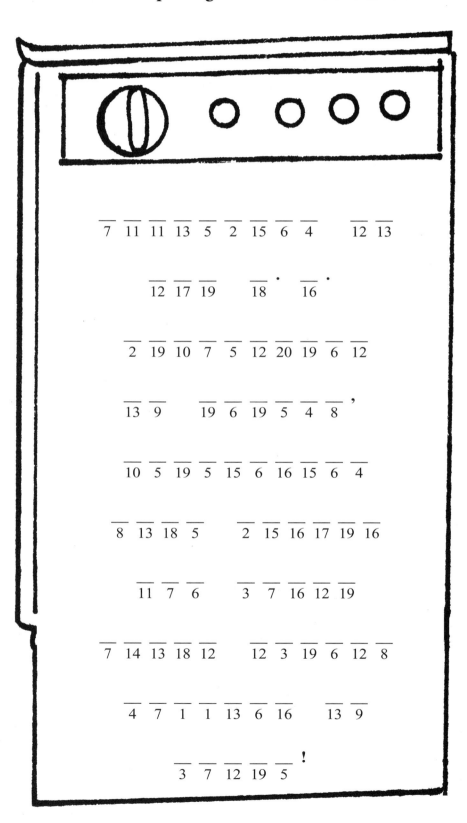

7 11 11 13 5 2 15 6 4   12 13

12 17 19  18 . 16 .

2 19 10 7 5 12 20 19 6 12

13 9  19 6 19 5 4 8 ,

10 5 19 5 15 6 16 15 6 4

8 13 18 5  2 15 16 17 19 16

11 7 6  3 7 16 12 19

7 14 13 18 12  12 3 19 6 12 8

4 7 1 1 13 6 16  13 9

3 7 12 19 5 !

14

# ECOLOGY LINK-UP

Can you place these ecology-related words in their correct spaces?

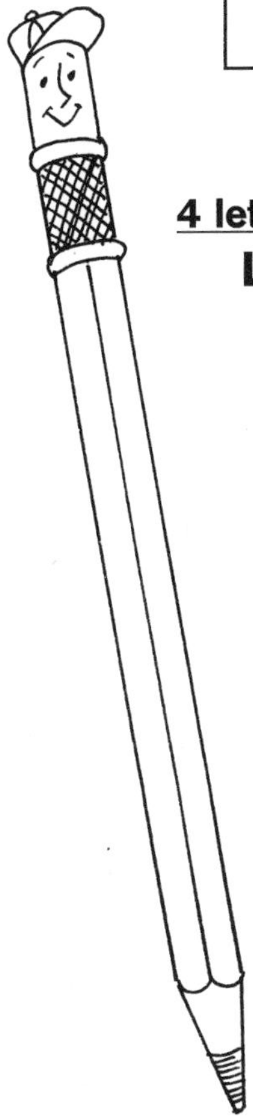

**4 letter word**
LIFE

**5 letter words**
OZONE
REUSE
SOLAR
WATER

**7 letter words**
CLIMATE
HABITAT
NATURAL

**8 letter word**
CONSERVE

**9 letter word**
BIOSPHERE

# FINDING THE ANSWER

**The process by which plants and animals take in oxygen and give out carbon dioxide is known as ...**

To complete the sentence above, travel through this flower maze to reach the correct final word.

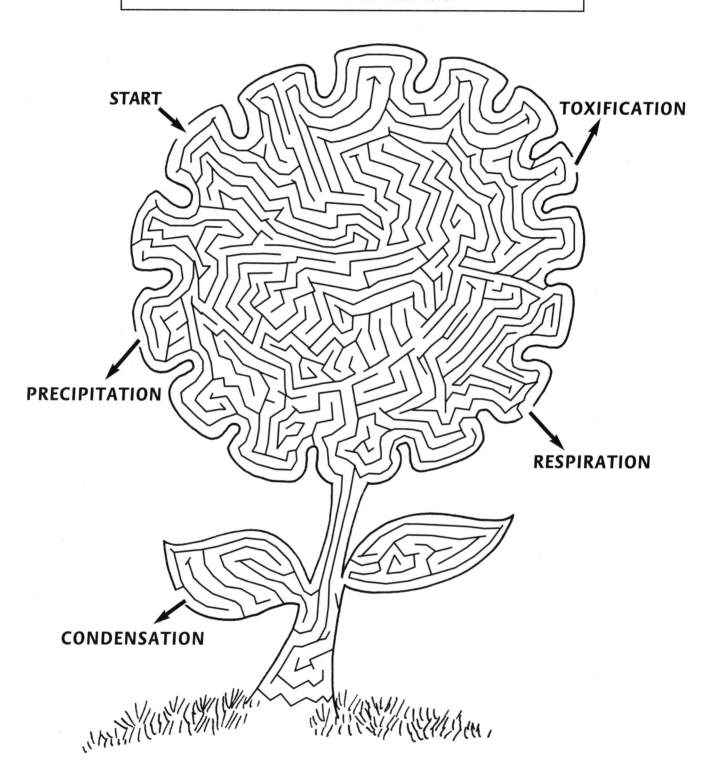

START

TOXIFICATION

PRECIPITATION

RESPIRATION

CONDENSATION

# FIND AND RECYCLE

**Recycling means taking materials from products you have finished using and making brand new products with them.**

Find and circle these items that a typical household can collect to recycle.

ALUMINUM SODA CANS ☐☐☐     BOTTLES ☐☐
DEFLATED RUBBER TIRE ☐     EMPTY PAINT CAN ☐
HANGER ☐     MILK CONTAINER ☐
NEWSPAPER ☐     TIN CANS ☐☐

# FUN AT THE NURSERY

**A nursery is a place where plants are grown and sold to the general public. It's a great place to start if you want a greener backyard!**

Find and circle the following objects in this funny nursery scene.

☐ ARROW  ☐ BANANA PEEL  ☐ BROOM  ☐ CACTUS
☐ DOG  ☐ DRUM  ☐ ENVELOPE  ☐ HEART
☐ MOUSE  ☐ RAKE  ☐ STAR  ☐ TURTLE

# GREEN PLANTS & THE SUN

**Green plants need sunlight to stay alive.**

Circle all the letters that contain a star ✪.
Then write these letters in the spaces below to
complete the last word of the mystery sentence.

| O E | ✪ P | ◎ T | ✪ H | ◆ R | ■ E | O H |
|-----|-----|-----|-----|-----|-----|-----|
| ◆ L | ■ P | ✪ O | O C | ✪ T | ✪ O | ◎ S |
| ✪ S | ✪ Y | ◆ U | ◎ M | ■ G | O T | ✪ N |
| ■ D | O G | ✪ T | ✪ H | ◆ R | ◎ L | ■ E |
| ◎ N | ✪ E | ◆ F | ◎ W | ✪ S | ■ Y | O D |
| ✪ I | ■ S | O A | ◆ M | ◎ N | ■ E | ✪ S |

MYSTERY SENTENCE:

The process by which green plants convert the energy
of sunlight into chemical energy is called

_ _ _ _ _ _ _ _ _ _ _ _ _ _ .

# LAWN MOWING TIP

**Did you know grass clippings are good for your lawn?**

To discover why, write these letters in numerical order (from 1 to 17) in the spaces below to complete the answer.

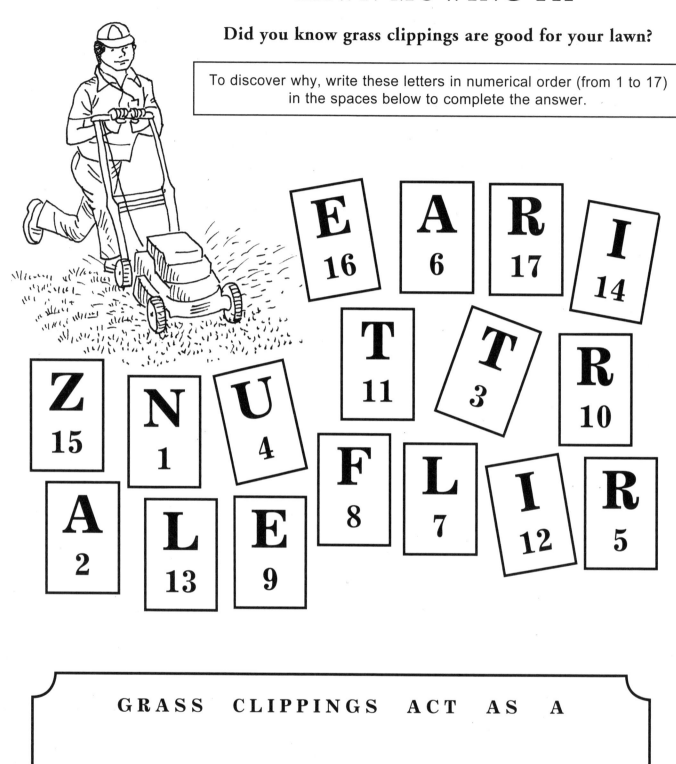

GRASS   CLIPPINGS   ACT   AS   A

___ ___ ___ ___ ___ ___ ___   ___ ___ ___ ___ ___ ___ ___ ___ ___ ___ .
 1   2   3   4   5   6   7     8   9  10  11  12  13  14  15  16  17

# MISSING VOWELS

These words are missing their vowels. Add the correct vowels (A, E, I, O, U)
with the help of these clues.

V R G R N - Plant whose leaf cover remains alive year-round

_ _ _ _ _ _ _ _ _

C L G S T - Scientist who studies ecology

_ _ _ _ _ _ _ _ _

X T N C T - A species that is no longer living on Earth

_ _ _ _ _ _ _

B C Y C L - Non-pollutant form of transportation

_ _ _ _ _ _ _

N V R N M N T - The conditions in which an animal or plant lives

_ _ _ _ _ _ _ _ _ _ _

R T H - Third planet from the sun

_ _ _ _ _

# ORIGIN OF "ECOLOGY"

**The word "ecology" was first used in 1866 by a German scientist.**

To learn the scientist's name, first find and circle the word "ECOLOGY" 6 times in this puzzle. The letters that remain, once listed below in the order they appear, will spell out the name.

| | | | | | | |
|---|---|---|---|---|---|---|
| Y | G | O | L | O | C | E |
| G | Y | E | R | N | E | C |
| O | G | S | T | H | C | O |
| L | O | E | I | N | O | L |
| O | L | R | I | C | L | O |
| C | O | H | H | A | O | G |
| E | C | O | L | O | G | Y |
| E | E | C | K | E | Y | L |

_ _ _ _ _      _ _ _ _ _ _ _

**WAS A ZOOLOGIST WHO WAS KNOWN FOR HIS
FREQUENT INVENTION OF NEW SCIENTIFIC TERMS.**

# PICTURE CROSSWORD FUN

Complete this picture crossword puzzle. The circled letters, once unscrambled, will spell out the final word of the sentence below.

— — — — — — — — — —
scrambled circled letters

ANY GROUP OF LIVING AND NONLIVING THINGS THAT INTERACT WITH EACH OTHER IS CONSIDERED AN

— — — — — — — — — — .
unscrambled circled letters

# POWER OF THE WIND

**Wind power can be converted into useful forms of electricity.**

Decode and complete this sentence using the code chart below.

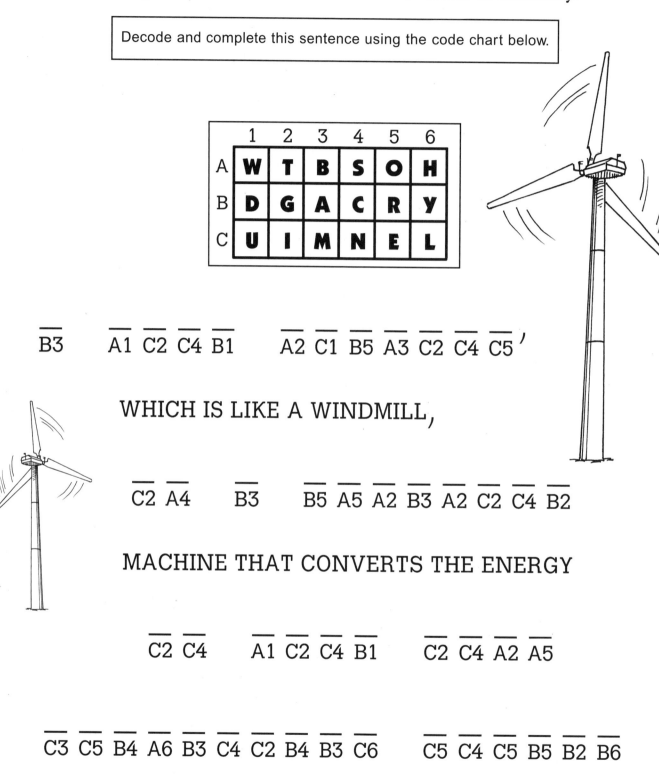

|   | 1 | 2 | 3 | 4 | 5 | 6 |
|---|---|---|---|---|---|---|
| A | W | T | B | S | O | H |
| B | D | G | A | C | R | Y |
| C | U | I | M | N | E | L |

$\overline{B3}$  $\overline{A1}\ \overline{C2}\ \overline{C4}\ \overline{B1}$  $\overline{A2}\ \overline{C1}\ \overline{B5}\ \overline{A3}\ \overline{C2}\ \overline{C4}\ \overline{C5}$ ,

WHICH IS LIKE A WINDMILL,

$\overline{C2}\ \overline{A4}$  $\overline{B3}$  $\overline{B5}\ \overline{A5}\ \overline{A2}\ \overline{B3}\ \overline{A2}\ \overline{C2}\ \overline{C4}\ \overline{B2}$

MACHINE THAT CONVERTS THE ENERGY

$\overline{C2}\ \overline{C4}$  $\overline{A1}\ \overline{C2}\ \overline{C4}\ \overline{B1}$  $\overline{C2}\ \overline{C4}\ \overline{A2}\ \overline{A5}$

$\overline{C3}\ \overline{C5}\ \overline{B4}\ \overline{A6}\ \overline{B3}\ \overline{C4}\ \overline{C2}\ \overline{B4}\ \overline{B3}\ \overline{C6}$  $\overline{C5}\ \overline{C4}\ \overline{C5}\ \overline{B5}\ \overline{B2}\ \overline{B6}$

# SAVING TREES

**Recycling one ton (2,000 lbs.) of paper saves the equivalent of 17 trees.**

How many times does the word TREE appear in this puzzle? Circle and count each one.

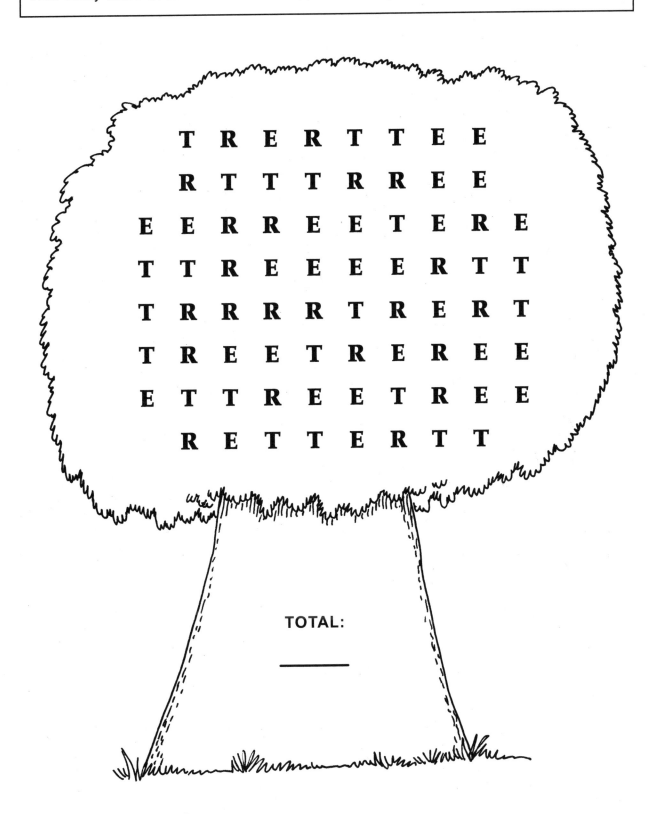

```
T  R  E  R  T  T  E  E
R  T  T  T  R  R  E  E
E  E  R  R  E  E  T  E  R  E
T  T  R  E  E  E  E  R  T  T
T  R  R  R  R  T  R  E  R  T
T  R  E  E  T  R  E  R  E  E
E  T  T  R  E  E  T  R  E  E
R  E  T  T  E  R  T  T
```

TOTAL:

_____

# SIFTING SAND BY THE SEASHORE

Our sandy beaches are wonderful places to visit and have fun. But they are also an important part of our ecosystem, as they support a variety of species and plant life.

Find and circle 12 things in this scene that begin with the letter "S".

# THAT'S A LOT OF TRASH!

Every day we throw away enough trash to fill about 63,000 garbage trucks. If this many trucks were lined up one after another ... the line would be almost 250 miles long! That's approximately the distance from our nation's capital, Washington, D.C., to which one of these major cities?

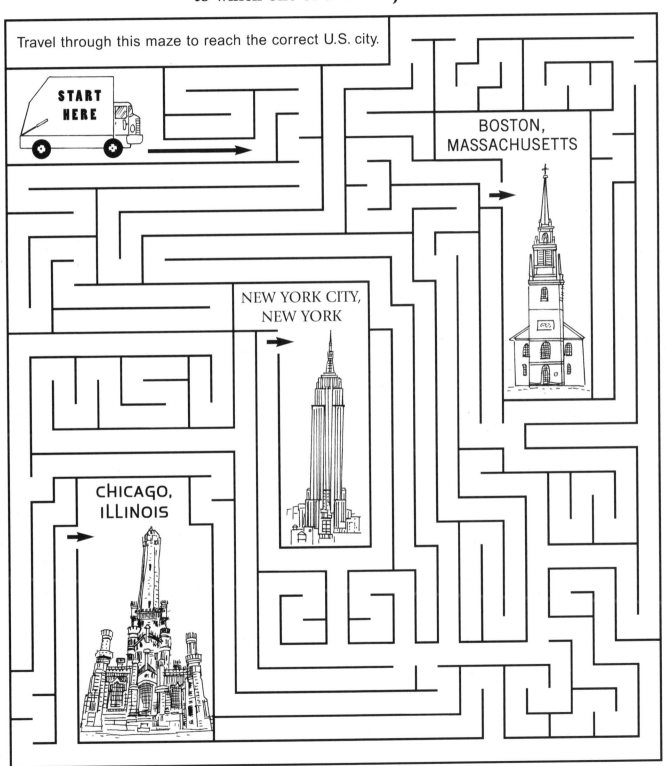

Travel through this maze to reach the correct U.S. city.

START HERE

BOSTON, MASSACHUSETTS

NEW YORK CITY, NEW YORK

CHICAGO, ILLINOIS

# THE LUNGS OF OUR PLANET

**The Amazon Rainforest covers over a billion acres in South American countries such as Brazil, Venezuela, and Peru. It continuously recycles carbon dioxide into oxygen. More than twenty percent of the world's oxygen is produced in the Amazon Rainforest!**

Circle and find 10 things that don't belong in this rainforest scene.

# THE SYMBOL OF RECYCLING

The recycling symbol is so familiar to us because it is seen on products all over the world. The symbol, used to designate recyclable materials, was designed in 1970.

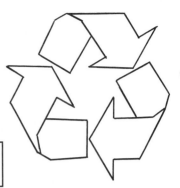

Correctly travel through this maze to discover the name of the designer.

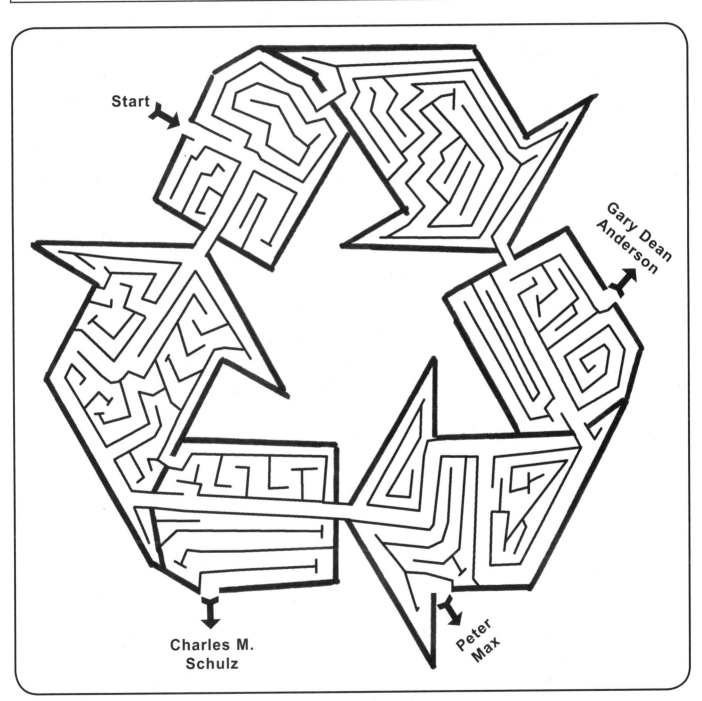

Start

Gary Dean Anderson

Charles M. Schulz

Peter Max

# THE THREE R'S

**If you remember the three R's, you will have all the information you need to help the environment.**

To learn the three R's, choose the correct path and travel through this maze.

START

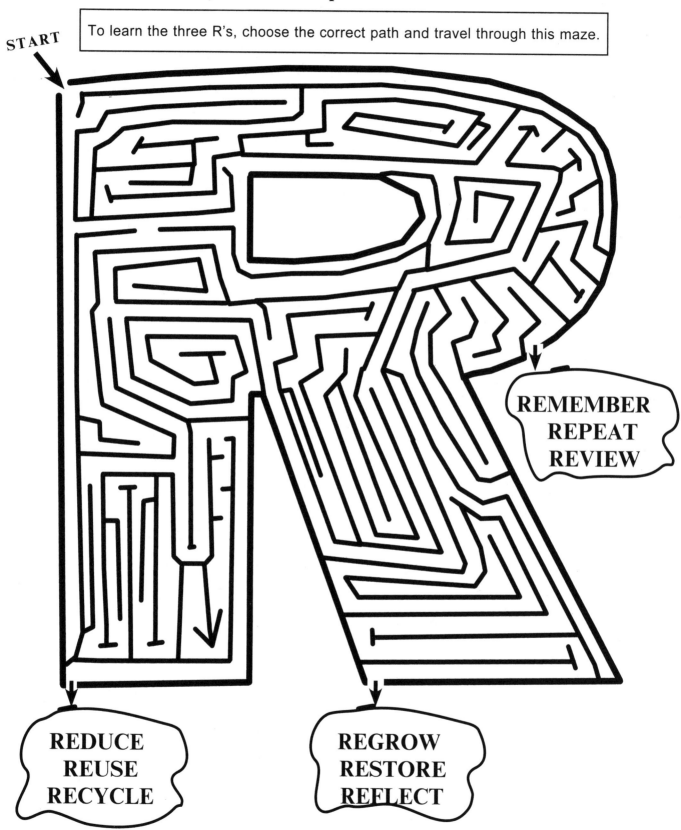

REMEMBER
REPEAT
REVIEW

REDUCE
REUSE
RECYCLE

REGROW
RESTORE
REFLECT

# TIME

**Do you know how long it takes garbage to naturally break down?**

Follow the correct path for each type of trash in this multi-part maze.

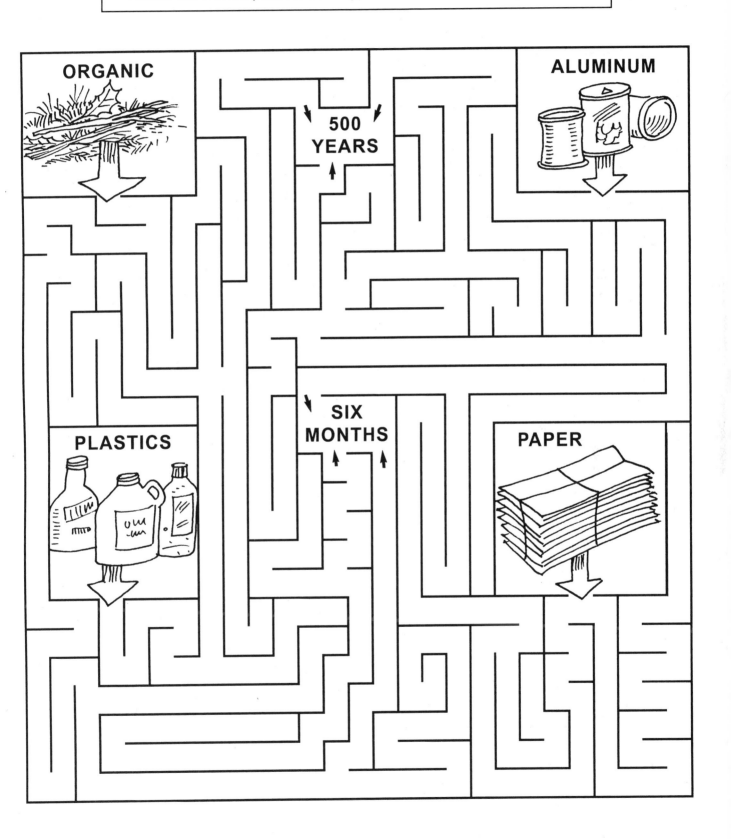

# UP IN THE AIR

**No one knows for sure how many birds in total there are in the world. It is estimated that there are about 10,000 different kinds. Over 1200 of those species are facing extinction.**

To learn how you can help keep our feathered friends around, first fill in the blanks with the missing words. Then write the numbered letters in numerical order in the blank spaces below.

RED, WHITE AND ____ → _ _ _
4 20 11

THANKSGIVING MONTH → _ _ _ _ _ _ _
3 5 24 13   8 16

A RED FRUIT → _ _ _ _ _
22 1 18 19 9

SATURDAY AND SUNDAY → _ _ _ _ _ _ _
6 21 15 23 7 17 12

OPPOSITE OF FAST → _ _ _ _
25 2 10 14

#1 _ _ A _ T F _ _ _ ERS AND TR _ _ S WHERE
  1 2   3     4 5 6        7 8

BIRDS CAN FIND FOOD AND MAKE HOMES.

#2 S _ T _ UT F _ E _ _ RS IN _ INT _ _
  9   10    11  12 13    14    15 16

WHEN FOOD IS SCARCE.

#3 DO _ 'T _ O L _ T _ L _ _ ES AND RI _ ER _ .
  17    18 19  20 21 22 23              24    25

# WASTEFUL GADGETS

People in the U.S. throw away about 400 million pieces of consumer electronic equipment (such as computers, cell phones, and personal music players) per year.

> To discover the name given to scrapped electronics, first drop a letter from each word in column A to complete a new word in column B. Write each dropped letter in column C to form the phrase.

| A | B | C |
|---|---|---|
| EASY | __ __ Y | __ |
| WINK | __ __ K | __ |
| HEAT | __ __ E | __ |
| SEVEN | E __ E __ | __ |
| START | __ T __ R | __ |
| NEAR | R __ __ | __ |

# WATER, WATER . . . EVERYWHERE?

The world's water exists naturally in different forms and locations - such as in the air, on the surface, below the ground, and of course in the oceans. In fact, water covers nearly three-fourths of the earth!

Unscramble these words having to do with water. (The clues can help.) Then write each of the numbered letters in their correct spaces below to complete the mystery fact.

**A E C F T U**
(You turn this to control flow of water)
— — — — — —
1  15  11  9  14  6

**A E S K L**
(Erie and Superior, for example)
— — — — —
   8     3  17

**P R A V O**
(Fog, mist, or steam)
— — — — —
   5     10  2

**R A I O T S R N M**
(Downpour)
— — — — — — — — —
7        12  4  16     13

## MYSTERY FACT:

— — — — H W — — E —
1 2 3 4     5 6   7

— — C — — — T S F O —
8 9   10 11 12         13

ONLY 2.5% OF THE

— — R — H ' —
14 15   16     17

WATER.

Conserve water by turning off the faucet while brushing!

34

# WHAT DO ECOLOGISTS DO?

**The work of ecologists is very important. Ecologists work in many different places such as universities, government agencies, and museums.**

Unscramble this list of "ecologist jobs" by writing the letter of the alphabet that comes BEFORE each of these letters below. (The first letter of each has been done for you.)

**#1  T** _

U F B D I   B O E

B E W J T F   T U V E F O U T .

**#2  G** _

H J W F   B E W J D F   U P

M P D B M ,   T U B U F ,

B O E   G F E F S B M

H P W F S O N F O U   B H F O D J F T .

**#3  S** _

T P M W F   F O W J S P O N F O U B M

Q S P C M F N T .

**#4  C** _

D P O E V D U   S F T F B S D I .

35

# SOLUTIONS

## A GLOBAL OBSERVANCE

Earth Day is celebrated in many countries each year on April 22. The day helps inspire awareness of and appreciation for our Earth's environment. The date is also important because it is the birthday of a famous agriculturist.

Travel through this letter maze by choosing the path made up of only letters from the phrase -
SAVE OUR PLANET
(Hint: The letters will be used more than once and will not appear in any particular order.)

George Washington Carver
Botany researcher & innovator of agricultural science

Julius Sterling Morton
U.S. Secretary of Agriculture & Founder of Arbor Day

Gaylord Nelson
U.S. Senator & Originator of Earth Day

START

Page 1

## A HIDDEN MESSAGE

Write these words in alphabetical order into the puzzle grid. The fourth letter of each word will help spell out a hidden message.

HIDDEN MESSAGE ↓

| | | | | | |
|---|---|---|---|---|---|
| STAGE | C | R | A | T | E |
| CRATE | I | T | C | H | Y |
| WHINE | M | E | R | I | T |
| TRIED | P | L | A | N | K |
| MERIT | R | I | S | K | Y |
| UNDER | S | T | A | G | E |
| PLANK | T | E | A | R | Y |
| ITCHY | T | R | I | E | D |
| RISKY | U | N | D | E | R |
| TEARY | W | H | I | N | E |

Page 2

## A NEW IDEA

Our landfills are filling up with old asphalt shingles (the material used to cover roofs of houses). To reduce the landfill waste, a few companies are recycling the shingles into a useful product.

Find and circle the following ten words (having to do with a home's roof) in the puzzle below. The letters that remain, once listed in the order they appear, will spell out the hidden phrase.

○ ASPHALT
○ COLOR
○ INSTALL
○ INSULATE
○ METAL
○ SLATE
○ SLOPE
○ STEEP
○ STYLE
○ TILE

| I | P | A | E | L | I | T | E |
| N | S | M | E | T | A | L | T |
| S | T | Y | L | E | V | A | A |
| T | E | I | N | G | R | H | L |
| A | E | M | A | T | O | P | U |
| L | P | E | T | A | L | S | S |
| L | E | R | I | A | O | A | N |
| E | P | O | L | S | C | L | I |

SHINGLES ARE BEING RECYCLED INTO:

P A V I N G   M A T E R I A L

Page 3

## A SPECIAL MESSAGE

Using a pencil, darken in the areas that contain a dot ● to reveal a special message.

Page 4

36

## A WARMER EARTH?

Earth has warmed by about one degree
Fahrenheit over the past 100 years.
The Earth might be getting warmer on its own,
but many scientists think that
things people do are causing this change.

What is the phrase that is commonly used to refer to
Earth's climate changes?
Answer each clue below. The circled letters,
written in the exact order they appear,
will spell out the phrase.

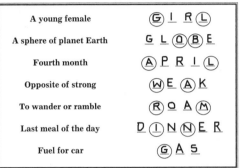

| A young female | Ⓖ I Ⓡ Ⓛ |
| A sphere of planet Earth | G L Ⓞ Ⓑ E |
| Fourth month | Ⓐ P R I Ⓛ |
| Opposite of strong | Ⓦ E Ⓐ K |
| To wander or ramble | Ⓡ Ⓞ Ⓐ Ⓜ |
| Last meal of the day | D Ⓘ Ⓝ N E R |
| Fuel for car | Ⓖ Ⓐ ⑤ |

## G L O B A L   W A R M I N G

Page 5

## ABSORBING POLLUTANTS

An average tree can absorb pollutants from the air - such as ozone and nitrogen
oxides. How many pounds of pollutants from the air can a typical tree
absorb in just one year?

Follow this number maze to add up to exactly **50** to reach the correct answer.

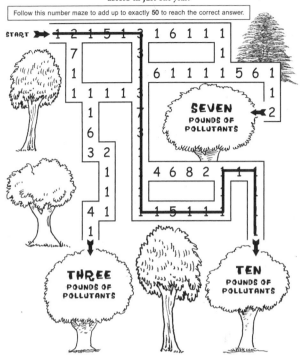

Page 6

## AN EARLY TREE

One of the earliest-known modern trees first appeared 370 million years ago!
It looked similar to a Christmas tree and quickly covered most parts of
the Earth with its first forests.

To learn the name of this tree, cross out each letter that appears **THREE** times in this puzzle grid.
List the remaining letters, in the order they appear, in the blank spaces below.

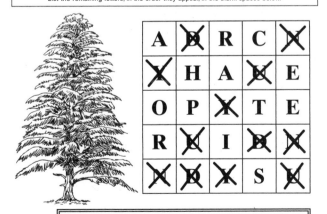

| A | ~~B~~ | R | C | ~~X~~ |
| ~~T~~ | H | A | ~~T~~ | E |
| O | P | ~~T~~ | T | E |
| R | ~~B~~ | I | ~~X~~ | ~~X~~ |
| ~~B~~ | ~~X~~ | ~~X~~ | S | ~~X~~ |

## A R C H A E O P T E R I S

Page 7

## AN INVISIBLE POLLUTANT

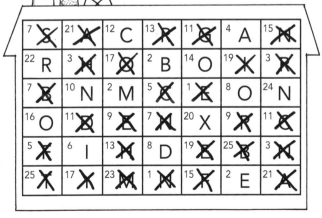

Smog hanging over our cities is the most familiar form of air
pollution. But there are different kinds of air pollution, some
visible ... some invisible!

Cross out all the ODD-NUMBERED letters that
appear in the boxes below. Then write the remaining
EVEN-NUMBERED letters, in the order they appear,
in the blank spaces. You will spell out the name of
an odorless, colorless gas.

| 7 ~~X~~ | 21 ~~X~~ | 12 C | 13 ~~X~~ | 11 ~~X~~ | 4 A | 15 ~~X~~ |
| 22 R | 3 ~~X~~ | 17 ~~X~~ | 2 B | 14 O | 19 ~~X~~ | 3 ~~X~~ |
| 7 ~~X~~ | 10 N | 2 M | 5 ~~X~~ | 1 ~~X~~ | 8 O | 24 N |
| 16 O | 11 ~~X~~ | 9 ~~X~~ | 7 ~~X~~ | 20 X | 9 ~~X~~ | 11 ~~X~~ |
| 5 ~~X~~ | 6 I | 13 ~~X~~ | 8 D | 19 ~~X~~ | 25 ~~X~~ | 3 ~~X~~ |
| 25 ~~X~~ | 17 ~~X~~ | 23 ~~M~~ | 1 ~~X~~ | 15 ~~X~~ | 2 E | 21 ~~X~~ |

Write the remaining EVEN-NUMBERED letters here:

## C A R B O N   M O N O X I D E

Page 8

37

## CLEAN AIR ON THE ROAD

Did you know that a car with a dirty air filter is more than just unhealthy?

To learn more, use this chart to decode the following fact.

| A | C | D | E | F | G | H | I | K | L |
|---|---|---|---|---|---|---|---|---|---|
| 12 | 4 | 20 | 13 | 6 | 17 | 2 | 19 | 15 | 7 |

| M | N | O | R | S | T | U | W | Y | Z |
|---|---|---|---|---|---|---|---|---|---|
| 3 | 16 | 8 | 18 | 11 | 10 | 14 | 1 | 9 | 5 |

T H E   G U N K   I N   A
10 2 13   17 14 16 15   19 16   12

C L O G G E D   A I R
4 7 8 17 17 13 20   12 19 18

F I L T E R   W I L L
6 19 7 10 13 18   1 19 7 7

C U T   D O W N   O N
4 14 10   20 8 1 16   8 16

G A S   M I L E A G E .
17 12 11   3 19 7 13 12 17 13

Page 9

## CLEAN ENERGY

Solar energy is energy from the sun. Today it is possible to capture the sun's heat and light and turn it into electricity, heating, and lighting. To discover the name of a device that can harness the sun's energy, follow the directions below.

Write the name of each of these objects. One letter from each word will spell out the name of a device which can collect and convert energy into electricity!

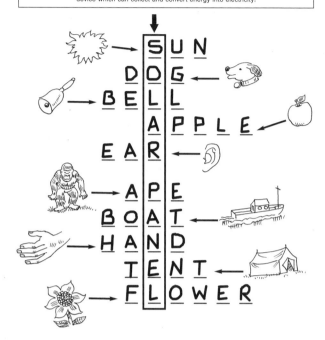

S U N
D O G
B E L L
A P P L E
E A R
A P E
B O A T
H A N D
T E N T
F L O W E R

Page 10

## COLOR OUR WORLD

Unscramble the names of these colors. A letter from each will spell out the hidden message.

| NMGAETA | M A G E N T A |
| WHTIE | W H I T E |
| VLOETI | V I O L E T |
| OELWYL | Y E L L O W |
| | |
| LGDO | G O L D |
| BOWNR | B R O W N |
| EIGEB | B E I G E |
| EDR | R E D |
| NPIK | P I N K |
| | |
| RONAEG | O R A N G E |
| | |
| REMCA | C R E A M |
| KKHAI | K H A K I |
| YARG | G R A Y |
| GERNE | G R E E N |
| BCKLAL | B L A C K |
| UELB | B L U E |

Page 11

## COMBO PUZZLE

Add the correct vowels (A, E, I, O, U) to these words. (The clues will help you.) Then find and circle the words in the puzzle below.

| E A RTH   D A Y | W I L D E RN E Ss |
| (April 22 observance) | (Natural environment not affected by humans) |
| R E CYCL I NG | TR E E s |
| (Reprocessing old materials into new products) | (Woody plants with branches) |
| N E BR A SK A | E n E Rgy |
| (U.S. state where Arbor Day originated) | (Kinetic, thermal or nuclear, for example) |

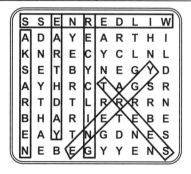

Page 12

38

## DID YOU KNOW?

Write the opposite of each of these words.
Then write the numbered letters in the correct spaces below to complete the sentence.

| | |
|---|---|
| WEST | E A S T |
| | 2 21 14 19 |
| LEFT | R I G H T |
| | 6 18 11 5 17 |
| TRUE | F A L S E |
| | 22 12 8 24 1 |
| OPEN | C L O S E |
| | 7 20 15 4 9 |
| TALL | S H O R T |
| | 13 23 10 3 16 |

THE E N E R G Y WE S A V E
     1 2 3     4

W H E N WE R E C Y C L E
  5       6 7  8 9

O N E G L A S S B O T T L E
10    11 12 13 14  15 16 17

I S E N O U G H T O R U N

A R E G U L A R L I G H T
                 18    19

B U L B F O R A B O U T
  20          21

F O U R H O U R S !
22      23     24

Page 13

## DISHWASHER FACT

Energy Star dishwashers, which use about one-third less water than non-Energy Star models, are designed to clean so well that prerinsing is not needed! Do you know someone who "cleans" their dishes before placing them in the dishwasher?

Use the chart below to decode the fact to the right.

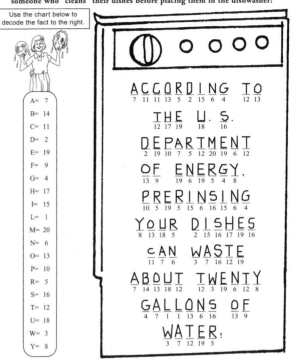

A= 7
B= 14
C= 11
D= 2
E= 19
F= 9
G= 4
H= 17
I= 15
L= 1
M= 20
N= 6
O= 13
P= 10
R= 5
S= 16
T= 12
U= 18
W= 3
Y= 8

A C C O R D I N G   T O
7 11 11 13 5 2 15 6 4   12 13

T H E   U. S.
12 17 19   18   16

D E P A R T M E N T
2 19 10 7 5 12 20 19 6 12

O F   E N E R G Y,
13 9   19 6 19 5 4 8

P R E R I N S I N G
10 5 19 5 15 6 16 15 6 4

Y O U R   D I S H E S
8 13 18 5   2 15 16 17 19 16

C A N   W A S T E
11 7 6   3 7 16 12 19

A B O U T   T W E N T Y
7 14 13 18 12   12 3 19 6 12 8

G A L L O N S   O F
4 7 1 1 13 6 16   13 9

W A T E R!
3 7 12 19 5

Page 14

## ECOLOGY LINK-UP

Can you place these ecology-related words in their correct spaces?

**4 letter word**
LIFE

**5 letter words**
OZONE
REUSE
SOLAR
WATER

**7 letter words**
CLIMATE
HABITAT
NATURAL

**8 letter word**
CONSERVE

**9 letter word**
BIOSPHERE

(crossword grid with words: CONSERVE, OZONE, CLIMATE, BIOSPHERE, REUSE, SOLAR, LIFE, NATURAL, WATER, HABITAT)

Page 15

## FINDING THE ANSWER

The process by which plants and animals take in oxygen and give out carbon dioxide is known as ...

To complete the sentence above, travel through this flower maze to reach the correct final word.

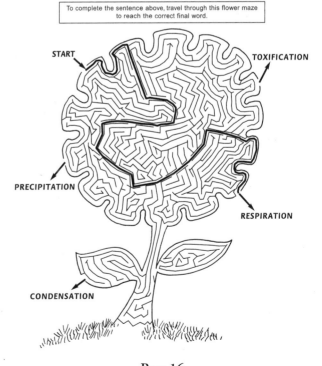

START
TOXIFICATION
PRECIPITATION
RESPIRATION
CONDENSATION

Page 16

## FIND AND RECYCLE

Recycling means taking materials from products you have finished using and making brand new products with them.

Find and circle these items that a typical household can collect to recycle.

ALUMINUM SODA CANS ☐☐☐   BOTTLES ☐☐
DEFLATED RUBBER TIRE ☐   EMPTY PAINT CAN ☐
HANGER ☐   MILK CONTAINER ☐
NEWSPAPER ☐   TIN CANS ☐☐

Page 17

## FUN AT THE NURSERY

A nursery is a place where plants are grown and sold to the general public. It's a great place to start if you want a greener backyard!

Find and circle the following objects in this funny nursery scene.

☐ ARROW   ☐ BANANA PEEL   ☐ BROOM   ☐ CACTUS
☐ DOG   ☐ DRUM   ☐ ENVELOPE   ☐ HEART
☐ MOUSE   ☐ RAKE   ☐ STAR   ☐ TURTLE

Page 18

## GREEN PLANTS & THE SUN

Green plants need sunlight to stay alive.

Circle all the letters that contain a star ✪. Then write these letters in the spaces below to complete the last word of the mystery sentence.

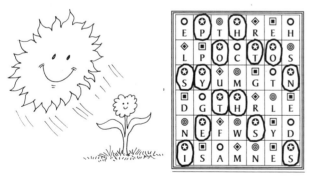

MYSTERY SENTENCE:

The process by which green plants convert the energy of sunlight into chemical energy is called

P H O T O S Y N T H E S I S .

Page 19

## LAWN MOWING TIP

Did you know grass clippings are good for your lawn?

To discover why, write these letters in numerical order (from 1 to 17) in the spaces below to complete the answer.

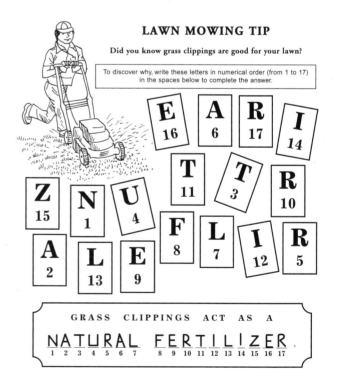

GRASS CLIPPINGS ACT AS A
NATURAL FERTILIZER.
1 2 3 4 5 6 7   8 9 10 11 12 13 14 15 16 17

Page 20

## MISSING VOWELS

These words are missing their vowels. Add the correct vowels (A, E, I, O, U) with the help of these clues.

V R G R N - Plant whose leaf cover remains alive year-round

E V E R G R E E N

C L G S T - Scientist who studies ecology

E C O L O G I S T

X T N C T - A species that is no longer living on Earth

E X T I N C T

B C Y C L - Non-pollutant form of transportation

B I C Y C L E

N V R N M N T - The conditions in which an animal or plant lives

E N V I R O N M E N T

R T H - Third planet from the sun

E A R T H

Page 21

## ORIGIN OF "ECOLOGY"

The word "ecology" was first used in 1866 by a German scientist.

To learn the scientist's name, first find and circle the word "ECOLOGY" 6 times in this puzzle. The letters that remain, once listed below in the order they appear, will spell out the name.

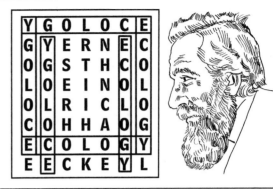

| Y | G | O | L | O | C | E |
|---|---|---|---|---|---|---|
| G | Y | E | R | N | E | C |
| O | G | S | T | H | C | O |
| L | O | E | I | N | O | L |
| O | L | R | I | C | L | O |
| C | O | H | H | A | O | G |
| E | C | O | L | O | G | Y |
| E | E | C | K | E | Y | L |

ERNST HEINRICH HAECKEL

WAS A ZOOLOGIST WHO WAS KNOWN FOR HIS FREQUENT INVENTION OF NEW SCIENTIFIC TERMS.

Page 22

## PICTURE CROSSWORD FUN

Complete this picture crossword puzzle. The circled letters, once unscrambled, will spell out the final word of the sentence below.

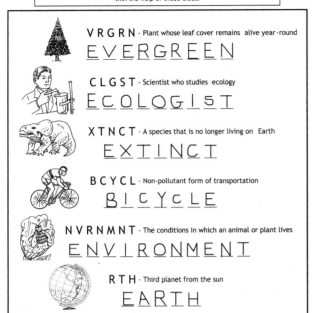

S T A R
C R A Y O N
M O U S E
C A R R O T
T R E E

S M C Y O S E T E
scrambled circled letters

ANY GROUP OF LIVING AND NONLIVING THINGS THAT INTERACT WITH EACH OTHER IS CONSIDERED AN

E C O S Y S T E M .
unscrambled circled letters

Page 23

## POWER OF THE WIND

Wind power can be converted into useful forms of electricity.

Decode and complete this sentence using the code chart below.

|   | 1 | 2 | 3 | 4 | 5 | 6 |
|---|---|---|---|---|---|---|
| A | W | T | B | S | O | H |
| B | D | G | A | C | R | Y |
| C | U | I | M | N | E | L |

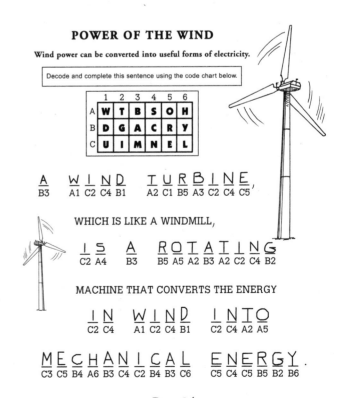

A     W I N D     T U R B I N E ,
B3    A1 C2 C4 B1    A2 C1 B5 A3 C2 C4 C5

WHICH IS LIKE A WINDMILL,

I S     A     R O T A T I N G
C2 A4    B3    B5 A5 A2 B3 A2 C2 C4 B2

MACHINE THAT CONVERTS THE ENERGY

I N     W I N D     I N T O
C2 C4    A1 C2 C4 B1    C2 C4 A2 A5

M E C H A N I C A L     E N E R G Y .
C3 C5 B4 A6 B3 C4 C2 B4 B3 C6    C5 C4 C5 B5 B2 B6

Page 24

41

## SAVING TREES

Recycling one ton (2,000 lbs.) of paper saves the equivalent of 17 trees.

How many times does the word TREE appear in this puzzle? Circle and count each one.

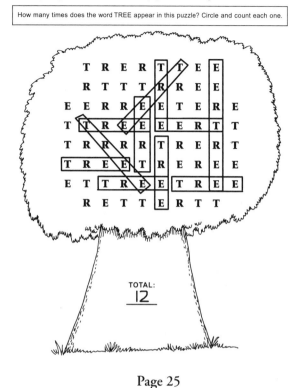

TOTAL:
12

Page 25

## SIFTING SAND BY THE SEASHORE

Our sandy beaches are wonderful places to visit and have fun. But they are also an important part of our ecosystem, as they support a variety of species and plant life.

Find and circle 12 things in this scene that begin with the letter "S".

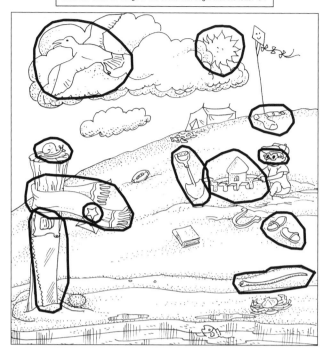

Page 26

## THAT'S A LOT OF TRASH!

Every day we throw away enough trash to fill about 63,000 garbage trucks. If this many trucks were lined up one after another ... the line would be almost 250 miles long! That's approximately the distance from our nation's capital, Washington, D.C., to which one of these major cities?

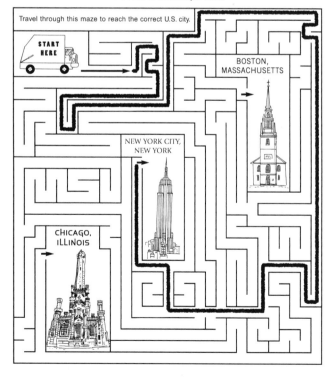

Travel through this maze to reach the correct U.S. city.

START HERE

BOSTON, MASSACHUSETTS

NEW YORK CITY, NEW YORK

CHICAGO, ILLINOIS

Page 27

## THE LUNGS OF OUR PLANET

The Amazon Rainforest covers over a billion acres in South American countries such as Brazil, Venezuela, and Peru. It continuously recycles carbon dioxide into oxygen. More than twenty percent of the world's oxygen is produced in the Amazon Rainforest!

Circle and find 10 things that don't belong in this rainforest scene.

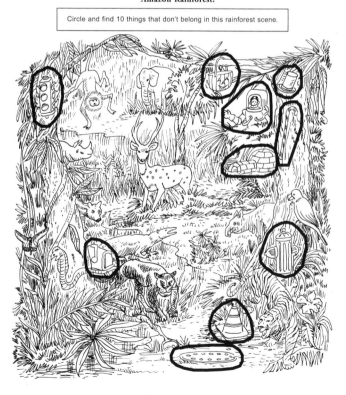

Page 28

## THE SYMBOL OF RECYCLING

The recycling symbol is so familiar to us because it is seen on products all over the world. The symbol, used to designate recyclable materials, was designed in 1970.

Correctly travel through this maze to discover the name of the designer.

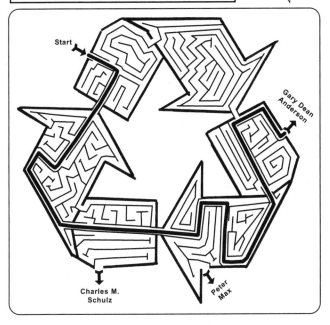

Start

Gary Dean Anderson

Charles M. Schulz

Peter Max

Page 29

## THE THREE R'S

If you remember the three R's, you will have all the information you need to help the environment.

START

To learn the three R's, choose the correct path and travel through this maze.

REMEMBER REPEAT REVIEW

REDUCE REUSE RECYCLE

REGROW RESTORE REFLECT

Page 30

## TIME

Do you know how long it takes garbage to naturally break down?

Follow the correct path for each type of trash in this multi-part maze.

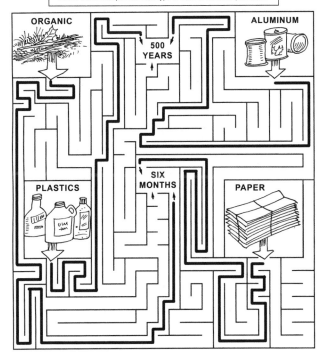

ORGANIC

500 YEARS

ALUMINUM

PLASTICS

SIX MONTHS

PAPER

Page 31

## UP IN THE AIR

No one knows for sure how many birds in total there are in the world. It is estimated that there are about 10,000 different kinds. Over 1200 of those species are facing extinction.

To learn how you can help keep our feathered friends around, first fill in the blanks with the missing words. Then write the numbered letters in numerical order in the blank spaces below.

RED, WHITE AND ___ → B L U E
                        4  20 11

THANKSGIVING MONTH → N O V E M B E R
                       3 5  24 13   8 16

A RED FRUIT → A P P L E
             22 1 18 19 9

SATURDAY AND SUNDAY → W E E K E N D
                      6 21 15 23 7 17 12

OPPOSITE OF FAST → S L O W
                   25 2 10 14

#1  P L A N T   F L O W E R S   A N D   T R E E S   W H E R E
    1 2 3       4 5 6             7 8

    B I R D S   C A N   F I N D   F O O D   A N D   M A K E   H O M E S.

#2  S E T   O U T   F E E D E R S   I N   W I N T E R
    9       10       11 12 13            14   15 16

    W H E N   F O O D   I S   S C A R C E.

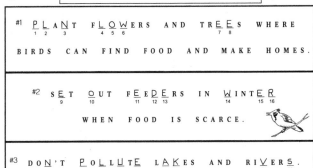

#3  D O N' T   P O L L U T E   L A K E S   A N D   R I V E R S.
    17         18 19 20 21               22 23           24 25

Page 32

43

## WASTEFUL GADGETS

People in the U.S., throw away about 400 million pieces of consumer electronic equipment (such as computers, cell phones, and personal music players) per year.

To discover the name given to scrapped electronics, first drop a letter from each word in column A to complete a new word in column B. Write each dropped letter in column C to form the phrase.

| | A | B | C |
|---|---|---|---|
| EASY | S A y | E |
| WINK | I N k | W |
| HEAT | T H e | A |
| SEVEN | E V E N | S |
| START | S T A R T | T |
| NEAR | r A N | E |

Page 33

## WATER, WATER ... EVERYWHERE?

The world's water exists naturally in different forms and locations - such as in the air, on the surface, below the ground, and of course in the oceans. In fact, water covers nearly three-fourths of the earth!

Unscramble these words having to do with water. (The clues can help.) Then write each of the numbered letters in their correct spaces below to complete the mystery fact.

| | | |
|---|---|---|
| A E C F T U (You turn this to control flow of water) | F A U C E T | 1 15 11 9 14 6 |
| A E S K L (Erie and Superior, for example) | L A K E S | 8 3 17 |
| P R A V O (Fog, mist, or steam) | V A P O R | 5 10 2 |
| R A I O T S R N M (Downpour) | R A I N S T O R M | 7 12 4 16 13 |

MYSTERY FACT:

F R E S H w A T E R
1 2 3 4   5 6   7

A C c O U N t s   F O R
8 9   10 11 12    13

ONLY 2.5% OF THE

E A R T h ' S
14 15   16   17

WATER.

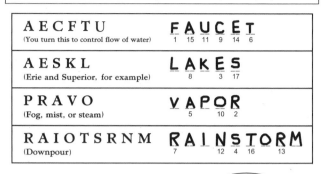

Conserve water by turning off the faucet while brushing!

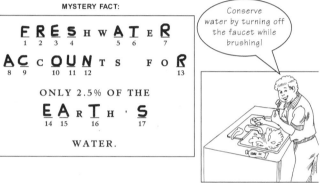

Page 34

## WHAT DO ECOLOGISTS DO?

The work of ecologists is very important. Ecologists work in many different places such as universities, government agencies, and museums.

Unscramble this list of "ecologist jobs" by writing the letter of the alphabet that comes BEFORE each of these letters below. (The first letter of each has been done for you.)

#1 T E A C H   A N D
   U F B D I   B O E

A D V I S E   S T U D E N T S.
B E W J T F   T U V E F O U T

#2 G I V E   A D V I C E   T O
   H J W F   B E W J D F   U P

L O C A L,   S T A T E,
M P D B M    T U B U F

A N D   F E D E R A L
B O E   G F E F S B M

G O V E R N M E N T   A G E N C I E S.
H P W F S O N F O U   B H F O D J F T

#3 S O L V E   E N V I R O N M E N T A L
   T P M W F   F O W J S P O N F O U B M

P R O B L E M S.
Q S P C M F N T

#4 C O N D U C T   R E S E A R C H.
   D P O E V D U   S F T F B S D I

Page 35